MAKING
HEALTHY
F O O D
CHOICES

Do You Know
What's In Your Food?

Neil Morris

Customer Service 888-454-2279
Visit our website at
www.heinemannraintree.com

Designed by David Poole and Geoff Ward
Printed and bound in China by South China
Printing Company

10 09 08 07 06
10 9 8 7 6 5 4 3 2 1

**Library of Congress Cataloging-in-
Publication Data**
Morris, Neil, 1946-
   Do you know what's in your food? / Neil
Morris.-- 1st ed.
      p. cm. -- (Making healthy food choices)
Includes index.
   ISBN-13: 978-1-4034-8574-8 (hardback)
   ISBN-10: 1-4034-8574-7 (hardback)
   ISBN-13: 978-1-4034-8580-9 (pbk.)
   ISBN-10: 1-4034-8580-1 (pbk.)
   1. Nutrition--Juvenile literature. 2. Food--
Composition--Juvenile
literature. I. Title. II. Series.
   RA784.M6255 2006
   363.8'63--dc22
                                    2006003972

Acknowledgments
The publishers would like to thank the
following for permission to reproduce
photographs:
Alamy Images pp. 23 (Photofusion
Picture Library), 35 (Tim Hill); Corbis pp.
9 (Picimpact), 10 (Owen Franken), 12, 13
(Jim Richardson), 19 (Anthony - Masterson/
PictureArts), 21, 24, 38 (Ed Lallo/ZUMA),
44 (AJ/IRRI), 46 (LWA-Stephen Welstead),
47 (Images.com); Empics pp. 11 (AP
Photo/Steven Senne), 31, 43 (Chris Young),
45 (David Cheskin); Getty Images pp. 4
(Taxi), 5 (Photodisc), 14 (Photographers
Choice/ Garry Gay), 15 (The Image Bank/
Peter Cade), 26 (National Geographic/ Bruce
Dale), 29 (PhotoDisc), 37 (Photographers
Choice/ Francesco Ruggeri), 39 (Sean Gallup/
Newsmakers), 40 (Photodisc), 42 (Stone/
John Lamb); Harcourt Education Ltd pp.
20 (MM Studios), 41 (Tudor Photography),
50 (MM Studios); Lonely Planet Images p.
30 (Greg Elms); Photolibrary.com pp. 17
(Foodpix), 51 (Foodpix); Rex Features p.
28 (Denis Closon); Science Photo Library
pp. 22 (BJANKA KADIC), 33 (DR. GARY
GAUGLER); Topham Picturepoint p. 48;
Tudor Photography p. 34; UPPA p. 36 (Miki
Yamanouchi).

The publishers would like to thank the
following for permission to reproduce
illustrations: pp. 6–7 and labels pp. 18–19
(USDA Center for Nutrition Policy and
Promotion).

Cover photograph of Cornell University
researcher Chengkun He examining
genetically modified rice plants, reproduced
with permission of Corbis (Jim Richardson).

The publishers would like to thank Nicole
Ann Clark RD for her assistance in the
preparation of this book.

CONTENTS

Any words appearing in the text in bold, **like this**,
are explained in the glossary.

ENERGY FOR LIFE:
You Can't Live Without It

Have you ever asked yourself why you need to eat and drink? Very often we eat just for pleasure, and we all enjoy our favorite meals. You probably have special treats sometimes, too. However, food gives us much more than pleasure. It is one of our most important basic needs.

This is because food is energy for life. We simply cannot live without it. Food provides us with the fuel we need for everything we do. This includes breathing, thinking, and even reading this book. It is no wonder that the choices we make about the foods we eat and the beverages we drink are very important. Being healthy depends on these choices.

▲ These teenagers need a lot of energy to enjoy a game of soccer.

WHAT ARE NUTRIENTS?

The substances in food that give us nourishment are called nutrients. They provide us with the fuel to be active, while helping us grow and keeping us healthy. The main groups of **macronutrients** are carbohydrates, proteins, and fats. We need large amounts of these, which are contained in different quantities in all kinds of foods. We also need smaller amounts of the **micronutrients** called vitamins and minerals. Two other important substances are water and fiber (see page 11).

▲ Fruit makes up an important part of a balanced diet.

WHAT ELSE IS IN OUR FOOD?

In addition to essential nutrients, there are many other things in our food and drinks. Some of these are okay in small amounts, but not so healthy in large quantities. Some unwanted **ingredients** may be contained in the original food source, but many others are put in when the food is packed, processed, or prepared. An example of this is the large amount of salt that you find in pre-prepared meals (see page 25).

It is important that you think and find out about what is in your food. Then you will be able to make educated, healthy choices about what to eat and drink.

FOOD GROUPS

In 2005 the U.S. Department of Agriculture brought in a new food guidance system called MyPyramid. The name MyPyramid was chosen because it takes a more individual approach to diet and food choices. The new pyramid's logo also shows a person climbing steps, to remind everyone of how important and easy it is to exercise daily.

The pyramid shows how we can put foods into six main groups, based on what they contain.

Choosing a wide variety of foods will help you have a balanced, healthy diet. Remember to eat lots of fruits and vegetables, whole-grain versions of starchy foods when you can (see page 11), and small amounts of fat, salt, and sugar.

▲ MyPyramid was produced by the U.S. Department of Agriculture to help people understand federal government food guidance.

GRAINS

Eat at least 3 ounces (85 grams) of whole-grain cereals, breads, crackers, rice, or pasta every day.

VEGETABLES

Eat lots of dark-green vegetables like broccoli, orange vegetables like carrots, and peas.

FRUITS

Eat a variety of fruits, but go easy on fruit juices.

OILS

Make sure you don't eat too much fat, sugar, or salt, and get most of your fat from fish, nuts, and vegetable oils.

MILK

Choose low-fat or fat-free whenever possible. If you don't or can't consume milk, choose dairy-free products like soy.

MEAT & BEANS

Choose lean meats and poultry. Remember that nuts and **pulses** are a good alternative source of protein.

KILOJOULES AND CALORIES

Scientists usually measure the energy we get from food in units called kilojoules (shortened to kJ). Many people use a different system of units, called calories (or cal), in everyday life. Since one calorie is a tiny amount of energy, they actually calculate in thousands of calories (called kilocalories, or kcal). To add to the confusion, they call kilocalories "calories"! Most food labels give both measures of energy, but health books and magazine articles usually stick to calories.

Quick conversions

There are about 4 kilojoules in 1 kilocalorie. To convert more precisely from one system to the other:

1 kcal (usually called a calorie) = 4.18 kJ

1 kJ = 0.24 kcal

BURNING CALORIES

We all use energy at different rates. Boys usually burn more calories than girls when doing the same things, because they generally have larger muscles. As a general rule, the heavier you are, the more calories you burn. Strenuous activities obviously use more energy than easy ones. However, you can see from the chart that all activities require energy, so you can exercise by helping weed the yard or by doing the ironing. Of course these are very general figures, because your individual number would depend on your weight and other factors.

Calorie burners

activity (for 30 minutes)	approximate calories (kcal) used
aerobics	200
basketball	230
cycling	190
dancing	140
gardening	160
riding horseback	130
ironing clothes	50
jogging	200
playing pool	100
inline skating	260
running	290
jumping rope	300
soccer	210
swimming	260
tennis	220
walking	120
weight-training	130

HOW MANY CALORIES PER DAY?

You may wonder how many calories you need to take in every day. This depends on many things, including your gender. It is affected by your height, weight, fitness level, and many other individual factors. As you can see from the activities chart, it also depends on your lifestyle. If you run often or play a lot of basketball, you will need more calories.

The chart below gives an average for different ages. If you record what you eat for a week, you will find that your calorie intake varies from day to day, but it usually averages out at these figures over a week.

► Extreme sports and activities, such as snowboarding, need a lot of energy.

How many calories (kcal) do you need per day?		
age	girls/women	boys/men
7–10	1,740	1,970
11–14	1,845	2,220
15–18	2,110	2,755
19–50	1,940	2,550

Carbohydrates are the most important fuel for energy. They produce about 4 calories of energy per gram of food, which is about the same amount of energy that proteins produce. Fats can produce more than twice as much (about 9 calories per gram), but it is important to get the right type of fats from the right kind of food (see page 10).

FATS FOR HEALTH

We all need some fat in our diet for energy and to help our bodies absorb important **vitamins**. Fats also supply us with essential fatty acids, which the body needs, but cannot produce itself. Many people think fats are unhealthy because they are so high in calories. However, this is not always so, and it depends which types of fat you eat.

◄ Olives, such as these, are pressed to make olive oil. This is a good source of monounsaturated fat.

Types of fat

✔ Some fats are much better for us than others. It depends on the chemistry. Fats contain various types of fatty acids. Fatty acids contain atoms of the elements carbon, hydrogen, and oxygen. Those fats with many hydrogen atoms are called *saturated* fats. Eating too much saturated fat can increase a person's risk of developing heart disease. Saturated fats are mostly solid at room temperature and include butter, hard cheese such as cheddar, and fatty meat such as bacon.

✔ Fats with fewer hydrogen atoms are called *unsaturated* fats and are generally liquid. Eating unsaturated fats can reduce a person's chances of heart disease. A fat with one unsaturated fatty acid is called *monounsaturated*, and good sources include oils from olives and rapeseed. Fats with more than one unsaturated fatty acid, like sunflower and soy oil, are called *polyunsaturated*.

WATER: AN ESSENTIAL INGREDIENT

Water is essential to our health, mainly because it makes up about two-thirds of our body weight. It is an essential part of blood and helps carry nutrients around the body. It also makes up urine, helping take waste products from the body. We need to replace the water that our body uses all the time. In a mild climate, you should drink about six to eight glasses (which comes out to 1.2 liters or 0.3 gallons) a day. In hot weather and when you are running around a lot, you need to drink more, because the body loses so much through sweating. This may sound like a lot of water, but remember, if you weigh 88 pounds (40 kilograms), about 60 pounds (27 kilograms) is made up of water. That comes out to 27 liters (7 gallons).

▲ Marathon runners take water from regular drinking stations during their long race. They are used to drinking small amounts on the run.

FIBER FOR DIGESTION

Fiber is mainly made up of the parts of plants that your body cannot digest. It is important because it helps you digest food. Fiber helps the body pass feces, or solid waste, easily. Whole-grain bread, brown rice, pasta, oats, beans, peas, lentils, seeds, fruits, and vegetables are all rich in fiber.

What do different foods contain?

3.5-oz (100-g) portion	carbo-hydrate (g)	protein (g)	fat (g)	fiber (g)	calories (kcal)
apple	11.8	0.4	0.1	1.8	47
baked beans	15.1	4.8	0.6	3.5	81
baked potato	31.0	3.9	0.2	2.7	136
brown rice	81.3	6.7	2.8	1.9	357
cabbage	4.1	1.7	0.4	2.4	26
cornflakes	89.6	7.9	0.7	0.9	376
eggs	1.1	12.5	10.8	0	151
jelly doughnut	48.0	5.7	14.4	trace	336
orange juice	8.8	0.5	0.1	0.1	36
plaice (type of fish)	0	16.7	1.4	0	79
plain yogurt	5.0	4.8	6.0	0	92
roast chicken	0	30.9	4.5	0	173
salted potato chips	52.9	7.0	34.6	4.5	536
spaghetti	74.0	12.0	1.8	2.9	342
whole-grain bread	31.8	6.8	2.6	4.5	171

CHEMICALS AND ADDITIVES:
Sometimes Useful, Sometimes Dangerous

We all depend on farmers and other producers around the world for our food. We like to think that it is all natural and healthy, but sometimes dangerous substances are used to help grow and produce food. These substances do not always appear on food labels, so we rely on our governments to watch over them for us. Over the years many dangerous substances have been banned.

Pesticides are chemical or **biological** substances that farmers sometimes spray on crops. They do this to prevent crops from being damaged by insects or diseases. Herbicides are used to kill weeds that compete with the crops for nutrients in the soil. Fungicides kill different types of **fungus**. The fungi are often in the form of **mold** or mildew and cause fruit to rot. People are used to buying healthy-looking, unmarked fruits and vegetables that are cheap. Pesticides, herbicides, and fungicides help with this, but there are possible problems. The danger is that traces of these chemicals might get into the **food chain** or damage the environment by staying in the soil or seeping into water supplies.

Scientists test all substances that are used on food crops, and governments set limits on the amounts that may be used. They also test food to see if any harmful substances are present. There are twelve different chemical substances that **environmentalists** and the United Nations want banned completely. They call them the Dirty Dozen.

▼ A farmer in Idaho sprays his fields with pesticide.
The chemicals kill insect pests and weeds.

▲ This farmer in Wisconsin injects his cows with a growth hormone. This increases the cows' milk production. Some experts believe growth hormones can have damaging side effects. Some countries ban farmers from using them.

DDT (dichloro-diphenyl-trichloroethane) is one of the "Dirty Dozen." It was first prepared by a Swiss chemist in 1939. It quickly became famous as a killer of mosquitoes, flies, and fleas that harmed animals and crops. However, scientists soon realized that DDT was beginning to appear in animals and humans who ate sprayed foods. DDT does the job, but it is too dangerous because in large doses it can cause cancer. It was banned in many countries. However, large amounts are still used in some parts of the world, mainly for killing mosquitoes.

Farmers use medicines to treat sick animals and prevent disease from spreading. **Antibiotics** are given to control infections. There is a worry that traces of these substances could get into the food chain. Governments and food agencies control the use of these drugs.

Hormones are substances made in your body that control things, such as your body's growth and development. Farmers can inject extra hormones into cattle to make them grow faster and produce more meat.

THE ORGANIC ANSWER

"Organic" describes farming methods that do not use pesticides or artificial **fertilizers** on crops. Chemical treatments on animals are also not used. Foods labeled as organic must come from land that has been farmed in this way for at least two years. However, if food products have only some organic ingredients then the food label must reflect that.

ADDING TO THE TASTE (. . . OR LOOK, OR SHELF LIFE)

Additives are substances added to **processed foods** and drinks to preserve them, keep them fresh for longer, or improve the way they look or taste. Some additives come from natural sources. Others are synthetic, which means they are made artificially in a laboratory. For example, the **antioxidant** vitamin C is a natural additive, while BHA (butylated hydroxyanisole), which is used as a preservative in some fats, is synthetic.

In the United States, colorings have to be labeled with a FD&C (Food, Drug, and Cosmetic) number. Food labels in the United States must also show the reason why an additive that acts as a preservative has been used—for example, "to protect flavor" or as a "mold inhibitor."

Additive groups

	purpose	example	found in
antioxidants	make foods last longer	vitamin C (ascorbic acid)	sausages
colors	give food a better color	curcumin (yellow color from turmeric)	margarine
emulsifiers and stabilizers	keep ingredients together	pectin	jelly
flavor enhancers	increase flavor	monosodium glutamate (MSG)	soups
preservatives	make foods last longer	sulfur dioxide	dried fruits
sweeteners	make food taste sweet without using sugar	sorbitol	soft drinks

▼ Many different colors are added to make candy look fun and attractive. You should find additives listed on the box or wrapper.

Sometimes an additive is used in one substance, and then that substance is used in many different foods. This happens with colorings. It caused a scare in 2005 about a red dye called Sudan 1. This is used in wax polishes, but is not allowed in food because it can cause cancer. However, it got into batches of chili powder and then into hundreds of different food products. The foods had to be withdrawn. The scare showed why so many food regulations are needed, and why governments run random checks on foods when they are produced or **imported**.

▲ Tap water is treated before it is sent through pipes to your home.

MOVING FAST

Food products move around the world very quickly. Just a month after the red dye crisis in Great Britain, chili sauces and oils were recalled across the other side of the world, in China, because they contained traces of Sudan 1. Then a few weeks later, the Canadian Food Inspection Agency warned people not to eat two particular brands of chili oil because they might contain the dye. The scares inspired a U.S. laboratory to develop a new test for Sudan dyes that makes sure they do not appear in food products in the United States.

In the news, March 2005

PURE WATER?

You may think the water that comes out of your faucets is pure H_2O, but this is not true. Before the water is piped from the treatment plant, a chemical called chlorine is added to kill bacteria. In some places a mineral called fluoride is also added to prevent tooth decay. Fluoride is generally used in toothpaste, too. Some people are concerned that they have little choice in the matter and are against such an additive. Special filters can be bought that reduce the amount of fluoride, and many people choose to drink bottled water.

15

WHAT'S IN A SLICE?

Bread is often called the "staff of life" because so many people rely on it as an important part of their diet. It is a simple food that has been enjoyed for thousands of years, and it is high on most people's shopping lists. However, bread is another example of a food that often has more in it than you think. Most grocery stores and bakeries sell a wide range of breads. Most are made from wheat flour, water, yeast, and salt. You can choose a long, thin stick of white French bread or a small, round loaf of brown bread. Both are full of carbohydrates, and bread also has plenty of vitamins, minerals, and fiber.

ADDED FAT

There are other things in bread, including fat. Fat is contained in wheat flour, usually up to 1.2 grams in plain white flour and 2 g in whole-wheat flour per 3.5 ounces (100 grams) of bread. A muffin can have more fat in it than a Snickers bar.

The amount of fat in different bread products	
Two slices of whole-grain bread	2 grams
Plain bagel	1.5 grams
Muffin	12–20 grams

Fat is added to some bread so that it stays fresh longer. Today's sliced loaves do not go stale as quickly as they used to. Producers call this "added value." Also bread with fat in it can hold more water and air inside. Because water and air are cheap, it is profitable to include more of them in bread.

You might find on the label of wrapped bread that the bread contains "hydrogenated vegetable fat." This is liquid unsaturated fat that has been turned into a solid saturated kind by heating and bombarding it with hydrogen gas. You might find **emulsifiers** listed, too, and some of these include hydrogenated soybean oil.

Scientists say there are health risks in eating too much hydrogenated fat. Bread manufacturers claim that the amount of fat in their bread is always clearly labeled on the packaging. This is true, and that is why it is always a good idea to read the label.

▲ Popular brands of packaged bread may contain more additives than you would expect.

Which bread is best?

✔ Whole-grain, whole-wheat, and brown loaves contain vitamins B and E, as well as a wide range of minerals. Ingredients are listed on labeled bread.

✔ Bread made with stone-ground flour retains more of its nutrients.

✔ Fresh-baked bread from a small bakery, where they make the bread themselves, is good because you can ask what they have used in the bread.

WHAT'S ON THE LABEL: ❓
Everything You Need to Know!

It is very important to know what kind of foods you should eat, but how do you find out what is actually in the food? How do you know how much **protein**, carbohydrates, fat—and additives—there are in your favorite foods?

Help is at hand! Food manufacturers have to give you certain types of information about what is in their products. The information is shown in a standard way, so that you can compare what is in different foods. The labels shown here are for a portion of macaroni and cheese. We have used colors to explain different sections, but you will not find the colors on real food labels.

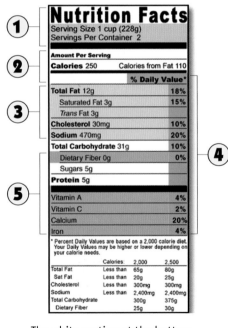

The white section at the bottom does not change from product to product. It shows recommended dietary advice for everyone.

① The green part of the label tells you how big a serving is. Measure out your food carefully to make sure you're getting the right amount.

Nutrition Facts
Serving Size 1 cup (228g)
Servings Per Container 2

Amount Per Serving

Calories 250   Calories from Fat 110

② This white part of the label shows you how many calories each serving contains. It also says how many of the calories are made up of fat.

▲ The U.S. Food and Drug Administration provided these labels and much of the information.

▶ Many people like macaroni and cheese, but do they know what it contains?

3

The yellow part of the label tells you how much fat, cholesterol, and sodium a single portion contains. Each of these can be bad for your health. It is best to avoid eating too much of them.

⚠ High percentages next to yellow labels are a bad thing!

	% Daily Value*
Total Fat 12g	18%
Saturated Fat 3g	15%
Trans Fat 3g	
Cholesterol 30mg	10%
Sodium 470mg	20%

4

The pink part of the label (the column on the right) shows you the percentage you get of the recommended daily amount of each nutrient. This is based on a 2,000-calorie diet. High percentages next to the blue part of the label are a good thing.

5

The blue nutrients are the ones that nutritionists encourage people to eat plenty of. Most of us usually do not eat enough of these, which is why it is a good idea to pick out foods that contain plenty of them.

Dietary Fiber 0g	0%
Sugars 5g	
Protein 5g	
Vitamin A	4%
Vitamin C	2%
Calcium	20%
Iron	4%

* Percent Daily Values are based on a 2,000 calorie diet. Your Daily Values may be higher or lower depending on your calorie needs.

DATE LABELS

Best before:

This date refers to food quality and flavor. It does not mean it will be harmful after that time. The date given will be accurate only if you store the food according to the instructions on the label. These might say "store in a cool dry place" or "keep in the refrigerator once opened." You might be surprised to learn that stores are allowed to sell foods after their "best before" date, as long as they are not a health risk.

WATCH OUT!

There is one food you should never eat after the "best before" date: eggs. Eggs can contain *Salmonella* bacteria (see page 33), which would multiply after the date.

Sell by/ display until:

You may see one of these next to other date marks. Some stores use them for stock control. They are instructions for store workers, not shoppers.

Use by:

You will see this date on food that goes bad quickly, such as meat and pre-prepared salads. It is very important. Never eat the food after the end of this date, even if it looks and smells fine. Otherwise you might get food poisoning (see page 32). If the food can be frozen, you can keep it beyond the "use by" date. Make sure you follow the instructions on the package, such as "freeze on day of purchase" or "defrost thoroughly and use within 24 hours."

smooth

USE BY:
SEPT 03 06

▶ Freshly squeezed pure orange juice will get gassy and sour much faster than juice with a lot of preservatives in it. Don't use it after the "use by" date.

▶ The information on food labels is in a standard form. This allows shoppers to compare different products and make their own choice.

STORAGE AND COOKING INSTRUCTIONS

The label instructions that give guidance on storing and cooking food and drinks are very important. You should always read and follow them carefully so that any harmful bacteria are killed and you avoid food poisoning (see page 32).

HEALTH CLAIMS

You might see a specific statement about health, such as, "Helps maintain a healthy heart." Most countries have laws that say such a claim must be true, but they do not have to be checked before claims can be used.

"NO SUGAR ADDED" VERSUS "UNSWEETENED"

A "no sugar added" label means that sugar has not been added as an ingredient. The food or drink might still contain fruit with a high natural sugar content, or it may contain milk, which contains a type of sugar called lactose. Some people cannot digest lactose properly, so some foods are labeled "reduced lactose" or "lactose free."

"Unsweetened" means that no sugar or sweetener has been added to the food. This does not always mean that the food has no natural sugar from fruits or milk.

The list of ingredients will tell you what sugars and sweeteners are in the food. The **nutrition** information will tell you how much sugar is in the food.

ORGANIC

Producers are allowed to label foods as "organic" if organic ingredients make up at least 95 percent of the product. If it contains more than 70 percent organic ingredients, these can be listed as organic in the ingredients list. Then the label has to show the total percentage (say, 80 percent) that is organic.

▲ These tomatoes were grown according to certified organic methods.

What do you think they mean?

✔ *Light* or *lite*
Many of the claims made on labels and packaging have more to do with advertising than nutrition. There is no legal definition of what "light" or "lite" means, but you would think it refers to reduced fat in chips or low sugar in drinks. To find out, take a close look at the nutrition label and compare it with labels on similar products. You might find there is less difference than expected. "Lite" chips, for example, might have two-thirds as much fat as other chips.

✔ *Value* or *economy*
Terms such as "value" and "economy" have no legal definition. What do they mean to you? Probably, good quality at a lower price, or a basic standard at a basic price? Again, compare the ingredients and prices yourself.

✔ *Fresh, pure,* or *natural*
These terms really mean whatever you take them to mean. Check out the ingredients and other label information and make up your own mind.

FISHY INFORMATION

Labels on prepacked fish must show:

- The name of the fish
- How it was produced (labels might say "caught in fresh water" or "farmed," for example)
- The catch area, such as "northwest Atlantic."

At the fresh-fish counter in a grocery store, you can look for this information on a sign next to the fish.

Many countries have tightened up their rules in recent years. In the United States, new rules introduced in 2005 say that sellers must show both the country of origin and method of production of all seafood. To make things simple, the Department of Agriculture decided that fish caught in open water could be labeled "wild" or "wild caught," but not "ocean caught," "caught at sea," or "line caught." They also said that fish could be called "farmed" or "farm-raised," but not "cultured" or "cultivated."

▼ In this market customers can ask the seller about different kinds of seafood or they can read the signs.

SEA FOOD COCKT
KING FISH STEA
TUNA STEAKS
PEELED PRAWNS
KING PRAWNS
1b BOX SQUID
5b BOX SQUID
SQUID TUBS
TIGER PRAWNS
NZ MUSSELS
FLYING FISH
HASSA
FROZEN SARDINES

MODERN CONVENIENCE:
Quick, Easy Food for Busy People

Years ago people spent a lot of time buying, preparing, and cooking food. This was mainly the job of the housewife of the family. Times have changed. Today most people lead very busy lives. They want all the modern conveniences when it comes to buying and preparing food. People like meals that can be prepared quickly and easily.

It is easy to see why convenience foods are popular, but they are also expensive. They usually cost much more than their basic ingredients. Surveys show that people like them because they save time and provide meals that many people feel they could not cook themselves.

▼ A convenient meal of chicken curry and rice can be bought in some grocery stores to be heated up at home.

In recent years pre-prepared meals and TV dinners have become much more popular. Most used to be sold frozen, but today many are chilled. They have been precooked by the producers and are ready to be heated up in the oven or microwave. It is very important to read the labels on pre-prepared meals and to compare different products.

SODIUM + CHLORINE = SALT

Processed foods and pre-prepared meals often contain a lot of salt, because it helps preserve them and improves taste. Many pre-prepared meals contain more than 2 grams of salt in a single portion. This is a big pinch, or a third of a teaspoonful. That might not sound like much, but the recommended daily salt limit for older children (over eleven) and adults is just 6 grams. For younger children, it is less—for babies, 2 grams; for four to six years, 3 grams; and for seven to ten years, 5 grams.

Salt, sodium chloride, is made up of sodium and chlorine combined together, which is another problem. Sodium is often listed separately on food packaging. We should aim to eat no more than 2.5 grams of sodium a day, because this is the same as 6 grams of salt.

Many people might think that they do not eat much salt because they rarely sprinkle table salt on their food. They do not realize how much salt is in foods, such as breakfast cereals, soups, sauces, and pre-prepared meals.

DANGER!

Sodium can raise your blood pressure. High blood pressure can lead to heart disease and problems with the brain's blood vessels.

Examples of salty foods

3.5 oz (100 g) of each food	salt (grams)
smoked ham	3.3
bacon	2.1
BBQ potato chips	2.1
cornflakes	1.8
cheeseburger	1.5
premade lasagna	1.0
salted peanuts	1.0
baked beans	0.9
canned soup	0.4

FAST-FOOD RESTAURANTS

Fast-food restaurants are also popular because they are quick and easy.
They usually do not offer many different foods, but you normally do not
have to wait. The food is delivered instantly or within a few minutes. The
idea started in the United States in the 1950s, and chains of fast-food
restaurants have since spread all around the world. The most popular
serve hamburgers, pizzas, or fried chicken, and most meals come with
French fries.

▲ A customer speeds a tray of fast
food to the table.

Some of these restaurants have been criticized by people who claim that
the food is of poor quality and too high in calories, salt, and saturated
fat. Nutritionists are worried that some people eat too much high-calorie,
high-fat fast food, which makes them overweight. They also point out that
this may be more a problem of quantity than quality—some people just
eat too much fast food.

Fast-food chains have been worried about bad **publicity**, but they are
still very popular and make a lot of money. Many companies now give
nutritional information on all their foods, so you can compare them and
make better choices.

How much fat and salt?

McDonald's has announced that it is planning to print nutritional information on the packaging of its famous burgers and fries. This follows complaints that the company is contributing to higher levels of **obesity**. Now you can immediately see how much fat, salt, and calories are in your extra-large burger.

The corporation said that the facts would be presented using an "easy-to-understand icon and bar chart format." It would include comparisons with daily recommendations for calories and nutrients. McDonald's hoped to have the new packaging in most of its 30,000 fast-food restaurants around the world by the end of 2006.

In the news, October 2005

CHECK THE WEBSITES

Another thing you can do is visit the different fast-food companies' websites. You can then compare statistics and decide for yourself.

The following list comes from www.mcdonalds.com. It shows how you can compare different items on the menu. Look at the difference in figures between the ordinary hamburger and the giant one, which is nearly three times the size and weight of the ordinary hamburger.

McDonald's nutrition facts for popular menu items

	serving size in ounces (grams)	calories	carbo-hydrates (g)	protein (g)	total fat (g)	sodium (g)	sugars (g)
Hamburger	3.7 (105)	260	33	13	9	0.53	7
Cheeseburger	4.2 (119)	310	35	15	12	0.74	7
Double Quarter Pounder® with cheese	9.9 (280)	730	46	47	40	1.33	9
Filet-O-Fish®	5 (141)	400	42	14	18	0.64	8
McChicken®	5.2 (147)	370	41	15	16	0.81	5
French fries (medium)	4.0 (114)	380	47	4	20	0.22	0
Bacon ranch salad with grilled chicken	11.2 (321)	260	12	33	9	1.00	5
Side salad	3.1 (87)	20	4	1	0	0.01	2

ROBOT FRIES

Some people do not like fast-food chains because their food always tastes the same. The reason for this is that production methods are similar all over the world. They often use a high-tech, automated way of preparing food. To cut costs, some producers use robots instead of people to produce and even prepare food.

▲ Cut potatoes flow along a production line at a frozen-food factory in Belgium.

Fries made by robots!

"Conveyor belts took the wet, clean potatoes into a machine that blasted them with steam for twelve seconds, boiled the water under their skins, and exploded their skins off. Then the potatoes were pumped into a preheat tank and shot through a Lamb Water Gun Knife. They emerged as shoestring fries. Four video cameras scrutinized them from different angles, looking for flaws. When a French fry with a blemish was detected, an optical sorting machine time-sequenced a single burst of compressed air that knocked the bad fry off the production line and onto a separate conveyor belt, which carried it to a machine with tiny automated knives that precisely removed the blemish. And then the fry was returned to the main production line.

"Sprays of hot water blanched the fries, gusts of hot air dried them, and 25,000 pounds of boiling oil fried them to a slight crisp. Air cooled by compressed ammonia gas quickly froze them, a computerized sorter divided them into six-pound batches, and a device that spun like an out-of-control lazy Susan used centrifugal force to align the french fries so that they all pointed in the same direction. The fries were sealed in brown bags, then the bags were loaded by robots onto wooden pallets."

Fast Food Nation by Eric Schlosser (New York: Penguin, 2002)

ADDED SUGARS

Nutritionists say we should cut down on added sugars rather than cutting out natural sugar in fruits and milk. Added sugars increase calories without giving nutritional value. They can also cause tooth decay. Look out for them in the ingredients list. They may be listed as sucrose, glucose, fructose, or maltose, as well as by other names.

Many processed foods are rich in sugar, so this is something else to check on the can or packaging. Desserts and bakery goods often have a lot of sugar.

▶ You will find added sugars in all sorts of sweet bakery goods, such as doughnuts. These foods tend to be high in fat as well. Nutritionists advise us to avoid too many "empty calories."

STREET FOOD

Early fast-food restaurants copied street-food stalls' way of selling hot dogs, burgers, and other foods that were ready to eat. This tradition still exists in many countries around the world. Street sellers often make their own food and help keep up local traditions. They can be a big tourist attraction, too. Hygiene standards, however, depend on each street seller. Sometimes it is easier to find out the food production standards of a big company than an individual street seller.

▲ This street stall in Mexico City offers a wide choice of traditional Mexican dishes.

Frozen foods pioneer

✔ Packaged frozen fish and peas were the first frozen convenience foods. Their great pioneer was an American named Clarence Birdseye (1886–1956). The company he founded still exists as Birds Eye Foods, famous for their frozen peas, fish sticks, and other foods.

✔ In 1912 and 1916 Birdseye took trips to freezing-cold northern Canada. There, people often froze food in the winter. After fish was caught, it quickly froze naturally in the snow. Birdseye noticed that when the fish thawed out later, it was still fresh and good to eat. By 1925 Birdseye was selling quick-frozen fish. Years later this became very popular when people started to buy freezers.

THE BEST CONVENIENCE FOOD IN THE WORLD!

You could say that the very best fast food in the world is fruit. It is easy to carry around with you, very quick and easy to eat, and does not need a knife and fork! Any kind of fruit should be everyone's first choice for snacks because fruit is so good for you. In addition to the nutritional value shown below, fruits are excellent sources of vitamins, especially vitamin C. Water makes up most of their weight.

▶ Tennis player Lleyton Hewitt enjoys a banana between sets.

Comparing fruits

3.5-oz (100-g) portion	carbo-hydrate (g)	protein (g)	fat (g)	fiber (g)	calories (kcal)
apple	11.8	0.4	0.1	1.8	47
apricot	7.3	1.0	0	1.8	30
banana	23.0	1.2	0.3	1.1	95
cherries	11.5	0.9	0.1	0.9	48
grapes	15.8	0.4	0.1	0.7	60
orange	8.5	1.1	0.1	1.7	38
pear	10.0	0.3	0.1	2.2	40
pineapple	13.0	0.4	0	0.5	52
raisins	69.0	2.1	0.5	2.0	272
strawberries	6.0	0.8	0.1	1.1	27

FRIENDLY AND UNFRIENDLY BACTERIA: ?

Are They Helping or Harming Us

Bacteria are tiny **organisms** that live almost everywhere. They are so small that they can only be seen under a microscope. Some live inside our bodies, in our intestines, and help us digest food. These are helpful, or friendly, bacteria, and many even destroy harmful organisms that would otherwise cause disease.

We often refer to harmful bacteria as germs. They are carried in food and water, and they use food in the same way as people—as a source of energy. They also cause food to spoil, or go bad. They do this by multiplying into large numbers and producing waste products, such as gases and acids. These wastes cause the unpleasant smell and taste we associate with spoiled food.

If you take in too many of these harmful bacteria or their waste with food, they can destroy your body's healthy cells. This can prevent your body from functioning properly.

WHAT IS FOOD POISONING?

Food poisoning is an illness caused by eating food that has been contaminated by harmful bacteria or other **microorganisms**. Often it causes vomiting and diarrhea. This helps your body get rid of the unfriendly bacteria.

A mild form of food poisoning generally causes no lasting harm. However, there are more serious forms. The bacterium *Clostridium botulinum*, for example, causes a very serious illness, called botulism. Its name comes from the Latin for "sausage," because that was the food it was first found in. The disease, which is rare today, is usually caused by eating canned meat or fish that has not been properly preserved.

There are hundreds of different strains, or kinds, of the bacterium called *Escherichia coli*. Most live harmlessly in cattle's intestines, as well as in our own. However, one strain, called *E. coli O157*, is fine for cattle, but not for us. Anyone who eats undercooked beef with *E. coli O157* in it can become very sick. It can cause kidney damage and other problems.

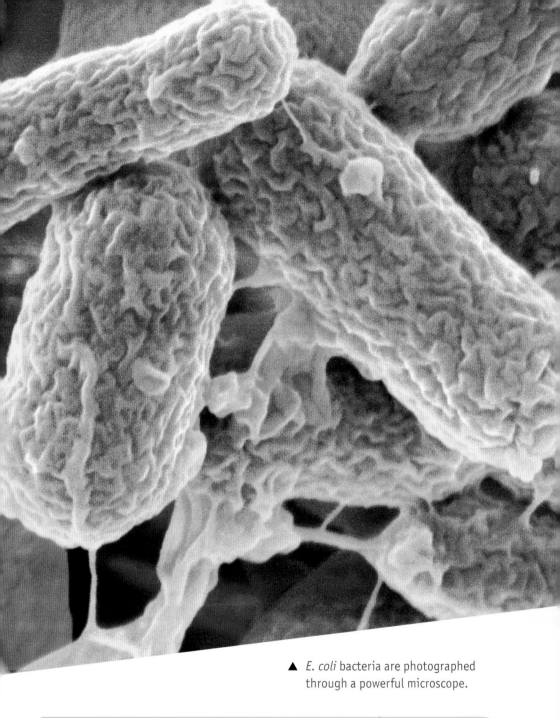

▲ *E. coli* bacteria are photographed through a powerful microscope.

DANGEROUS STRAIN!

Various strains of *Salmonella* bacteria can cause illness in humans. They are most often found in poultry, eggs, and unpasteurized milk (see page 37). If the bacteria are present in a food, they multiply quickly unless it is kept chilled. This is why it is good to keep these foods in the refrigerator.

STOPPING THE SPREAD OF BACTERIA

Bacteria can easily spread from one food to another if you are not careful. Take raw chicken, for example. If you do not wrap it properly when you store it in the refrigerator, the bacteria could spread to other food, either by touching it or dripping onto food below. After you have put the chicken in the refrigerator or taken it out, your hands could spread the bacteria onto anything you touch. Next comes the cutting board you rest the chicken on and the knife you cut it up with. Finally, if you put the raw chicken next to other cooked food on a grill, the bacteria would have their last chance to spread before being killed by heat.

Basic rules when handling meat

✔ Store raw chicken and meat on the bottom shelf of the refrigerator, so that it does not touch or drip onto other foods.

✔ Wash your hands thoroughly with warm, soapy water after you have touched any raw meat. It is a good idea to keep your fingernails trimmed and clean and to cover any cuts or grazes on your hands with a waterproof bandage.

✔ Dry your hands well using a disposable kitchen towel or hand dryer.

✔ Wash cutting boards, knives, tongs, and any other utensils in warm, soapy water. Wash them as soon as possible after you use them, and certainly before using them with other foods.

✔ Do not put raw chicken next to cooked food on a grill or barbecue.

▼ You must always wash your hands thoroughly with soap and warm water before and after handling meat and other food.

Cooking meat thoroughly destroys bacteria. The easiest way to check that meat is cooked is to use a thermometer. Today you can get digital food thermometers, probes for the oven and microwave, and even special barbecue forks. These are very useful for food caterers and restaurants.

Minimum temperatures for cooking meat

meat	minimum temperature
joints/cuts of beef, veal, lamb	145 °F (63 °C)
ground beef, pork, veal, lamb	160 °F (71 °C)
bacon, ham, pork	160 °F (71 °C)
stews, casseroles, leftovers	165 °F (74 °C)

HELPFUL BACTERIA

Milk is turned into yogurt by adding two kinds of bacteria: *Lactobacillus bulgaricus* and *Streptococcus thermophilus*. These bacterium change lactose (the sugar in milk) into lactic acid, which in turn makes the milk **ferment** and thicken. Several producers sell "probiotic" yogurt with live "friendly" bacteria. These are supposed to help keep a good balance of bacteria in the intestine. Many nutritionists believe that the new strains of bacteria advertised by certain brands are no more beneficial than those found in any other live yogurts.

▶ Fresh raspberries add a delicious touch to plain yogurt.

OLD PRESERVING METHODS

Since ancient times, meat and fish have been preserved by smoking, drying, or salting. All these tried and tested methods of preserving food remove water and slow the growth of microorganisms. They work very well, but they are not as popular as they used to be because they affect the taste and texture. Also many people are trying to reduce the amount of salt they eat (see page 25). Special foods, such as salt pork and salt cod, are still popular in many parts of the world. In Portugal people call salt cod their "faithful friend" because it is so reliable and nourishing. In South Africa people love dried salted meat called biltong. They put slices on bread or in salad, or they eat it on its own.

▲ In Vietnam these fish have been placed in rattan baskets to dry in the sun. Drying preserves the fish.

IRRADIATION

Other words to look out for on food labels are "irradiated" or "treated with ionizing radiation." This is a modern method of preserving. It bombards food with beams of radiation (energy in the form of light or heat), such as X-rays, gamma rays, or electron beams. The radiation kills insects, bacteria, or any other germs that may be on the food. Manufacturers like irradiation because it prolongs shelf life, and scientists say that it is safe. Some people believe it is dangerous and associate it with harmful **radioactivity**. In most countries irradiation is used only on a small range of foods. Chicken, pork, fruits, vegetables, juice, spices, and sprouting seeds are some of the types of food that can be irradiated.

SAFE MILK

Do you know the difference between pasteurized, sterilized, and UHT milk? They have all been heated to destroy harmful bacteria and make them safe to drink. The first process is named after the French scientist Louis Pasteur (1822–1895). He discovered that bacteria spread diseases, but that bacteria can be controlled.

Pasteurized milk is heated to between 145 °F (63 °C) and 151 °F (66 °C) for 30 minutes, or often to at least 161 °F (71.7 °C) for at least fifteen seconds. It is then cooled to less than 50 °F (10 °C). Sterilized and UHT (ultra high temperature) milk are sometimes called long-life milk. They are heated to even higher temperatures and last for months unopened. In some countries, you can buy unpasteurized milk and cream. If you choose these, make sure that you keep them properly refrigerated and that you do not keep them long.

▼ Chefs prepare food in a modern restaurant kitchen. Good standards of hygiene are extremely important in any kitchen.

FOOD DANGERS:
The Problems of Diseases and Allergies

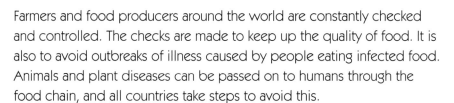

Farmers and food producers around the world are constantly checked and controlled. The checks are made to keep up the quality of food. It is also to avoid outbreaks of illness caused by people eating infected food. Animals and plant diseases can be passed on to humans through the food chain, and all countries take steps to avoid this.

Mad cow disease is the common name for a disease in adult cattle, called bovine spongiform encephalopathy (or BSE for short). BSE is a brain disease, and scientists believe it may have started in sheep. It spread to cows when they were given feed that contained meat-and-bone meal from diseased sheep. The first "mad cows" were identified in the United Kingdom in 1986, and the disease spread rapidly. At first many experts believed the disease would not spread to humans, even if they ate meat or drank milk from infected cows. However, steps were taken to stop the disease by checking animals and destroying infected ones.

Most cases of BSE in cows have been found in the UK and other European countries, but twenty cases have also been reported in Japan, four in Canada, and two in the United States.

▼ An inspector checks meat hanging in a slaughterhouse in Kansas. Controls have been increased everywhere since the discovery of BSE.

The prion problem

Scientists believe that BSE affects microscopic (very tiny) protein particles called prions. Animals die from a buildup of abnormal prions in the brain. Research is going on to find out more about prions, including how they become abnormal and possibly cause BSE.

In 1996, ten years after the outbreak of mad cow disease, British scientists said that they thought a human illness might be caused by eating BSE-infected beef. This was a form of Creutzfeldt-Jakob disease (or CJD), which was named after two German scientists who first described it in the 1920s. Experts called this new form variant CJD (or vCJD). Like BSE in cattle, vCJD is fatal in humans. There have been 180 reported deaths from vCJD. Its discovery led to further controls on cattle to stop the disease from spreading. However, it is still not absolutely certain that vCJD is always caused by eating BSE-infected beef.

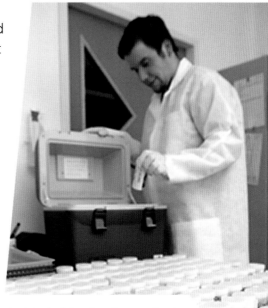

▲ A technician in a German food laboratory checks for BSE in brain samples from slaughtered cows.

WHAT IS BEING DONE?

Farmers were banned from feeding meat-and-bone meal to cattle. Then slaughterhouses were told to remove the parts of animals that were most dangerous for people. These included an animal's brain and spinal cord. In 1996, after the discovery of vCJD, British cattle more than 30 months old were not allowed to enter the food chain. In 2005 this rule was relaxed because there were so few cases of BSE. In the UK cattle older than 30 months must be tested before being allowed to be used as food.

All countries are concerned about BSE and CJD. The U.S. government, for example, does not allow its citizens to donate blood if they spent more than three months in the UK between 1980 and 1996. All countries have strict rules about cattle feed as well as about the movement and importation of cows and beef.

39

SENSITIVITY TO CERTAIN FOODS

You may suffer from food intolerance, which means that a certain food makes you feel sick. One of the most common causes of food intolerance is lactose (milk sugar). A food allergy is much more serious than an intolerance. If you eat something to which you are allergic, your immune system goes into action. This system is your defense against anything that might cause illness. The substance in food that causes the allergic reaction is called an allergen, and this is always a protein.

The allergic reaction may occur within minutes of eating the food or several hours later. Symptoms include itchy skin, nausea, and diarrhea. These symptoms are irritating rather than life-threatening, but some people with a severe allergy may have trouble breathing or may even lose consciousness. They need urgent medical attention. People with a severe allergy often wear a bracelet that gives details of it, so that doctors know exactly what to do in case of an emergency.

Do not just assume you have an allergy and avoid certain foods. Get any problem checked out by a doctor. Otherwise you might be missing out on essential nutrients.

▼ This bowl of tree nuts includes walnuts, hazelnuts, and Brazil nuts. Some people are allergic to one or more of these. They must read food labels carefully for traces of nuts.

WOW!

In 2004 the U.S. Congress passed legislation that requires all companies to create clear labels for foods that contain any of the eight most common food allergens: wheat, soy, milk, fish, shellfish, eggs, peanuts, and tree nuts.

Common allergens	Where you might find them
peanuts and tree nuts	breakfast cereals, cookies, cakes, candy, ice cream
eggs	pasta, soups, cakes, cookies, pastries
milk	bread, cookies, cakes, soups, sauces, margarine
gluten (the allergenic component of wheat)	bread, pasta, pizza, cakes, cookies, cereals, sausages, soups, ketchup

▲ This shows a range of gluten-free foods. They are clearly labeled.

GLUTEN

Gluten (Latin for "glue") is a sticky substance made up of two proteins. It is present in cereals, especially wheat, and helps make bread dough elastic. People who suffer from celiac disease ("disease of the abdomen") are sensitive to gluten. If they eat it, the gluten damages the lining of their intestine, and this stops their body from absorbing nutrients properly. There is no known cure for the disease, so sufferers must avoid eating anything containing gluten. This means they should read food labels very carefully.

CHANGING FOOD GENES:
New Developments in a High-Tech World

All plants and animals, and so all the food we eat, carry biological sets of instructions within their cells. These coded instructions are carried by **genes**, the basic units of **heredity**. They pass the code on to the next generation. In recent years scientists have learned how to change an organism's genes. This is called genetic modification, and genetically modified (GM) foods are already for sale in our supermarkets.

Genes are made of a substance called **DNA**. When the DNA of a plant or an animal is altered by humans, it is known as a genetically modified organism (or GMO). The process of genetic modification allows scientists in a laboratory to insert a single gene, or a number of genes, into an organism. This can change the characteristics of the organism. It could, for example, make it more resistant to certain pests or increase its rate of growth.

This new science can be used to affect whole crops, making them stronger and often producing larger **yields**. It was estimated in 2004 that seven million farmers were already growing GM crops. The biggest GM-producing countries are the United States, Argentina, Canada, China, Brazil, and South Africa. Favorite GM crops are soybeans, corn, and rapeseed.

▶ A scientist takes seed samples from a field of wheat. Many farmers in North America, and especially Canada, have opposed GM wheat. They fear that importers in Europe and Japan will not buy GM cereals.

▲ Protesters let others
know what they think about
genetic modification.

ENVIRONMENTAL CONCERNS

Many environmentalists are against GM foods. They say that GM crops
are unnatural, man-made organisms that may turn out to be dangerous to
both the environment and human health. According to the environmental
group Greenpeace, "Once these man-made organisms are released
into the environment and the food chain there is no way of recalling
them, and no one knows what the long-term effects of GM crops on the
environment and health will be."

Arguments for and against

Many people feel very strongly about GM crops, either for or against. Here are some
of the arguments. What is your opinion?

Reasons FOR
GM foods could:

✔ be more resistant to pests by having special genes introduced, and this could
   lead to less use of pesticides

✔ help the developing world by increasing harvests

✔ lower food costs by increasing yields

✔ benefit health by being enriched with nutrients

✔ improve taste, shelf life, and other food characteristics.

Reasons AGAINST
GM foods could:

✘ spread to non-GM crops and wipe out natural species

✘ reduce biodiversity (the world's wide range of plants and animals)

✘ leave farmers in the hands of a few giant companies that control GM seeds. (Many
   GM plants do not produce seeds, so farmers have to keep buying new seeds.)

✘ have health risks that at present are unknown.

▲ Samples of GM golden rice
  are grown in glass flasks in
  a laboratory in the Philippines.

GOLDEN RICE

In 2001 Swiss and German scientists inserted three extra genes into rice. Rice is one of the world's most important foods. This genetic modification made the rice plant produce a substance called beta-carotene. The rice grains took on a golden color. When we eat beta-carotene, our bodies turn it into vitamin A, which is important for human health. Any severe lack of vitamin A can lead to sight problems and even blindness. About 250 million of the world's people are deficient in (lacking) vitamin A.

The scientists claimed that golden rice has great nutritional value and could prevent blindness in children in developing countries. Golden rice seeds were distributed for free in parts of Asia and Africa. Other scientists have pointed out that undernourished people in those parts of the world do not absorb beta-carotene well. This is because their diet does not contain enough of the other nutrients that are needed to absorb vitamin A. It is very important for them to have a balanced diet. Perhaps golden rice is not such a wonderful solution after all.

PROCESSING AIDS

GMOs can be used to produce our food without actually being in the food. Then they are called GM processing aids. A good example is cheese-making, which uses rennet to **curdle** milk. Natural rennet comes from the stomachs of young calves, which makes cheese unsuitable for vegetarians. The important substance in rennet is called chymosin. Scientists can now insert a gene into bacteria so that they produce chymosin. This makes the bacteria GM, but they are not part of the cheese, which has no GM content. You might see these varieties called "vegetarian cheese" in some grocery stores. They do not have to be labeled GM.

GMOS IN THE FISH FARM

Only a few countries have allowed GM animals to be produced as food, but the technology is already there. One of the first GM species may be "super salmon." These fish have genes from a flat fish called a flounder introduced into their eggs, which make them grow much faster than normal. At eighteen months these GM fish can be five times the size of the natural variety.

As with plants, there may be dangers. Environmentalists say that the GM fish may escape into the wild and wipe out natural salmon, which are already under threat for other reasons. Other people simply do not like the idea that the fish they eat might contain genes from other species.

▼ Workers check salmon at a fish farm in Scotland. Scotland is famous for its high-quality salmon.

CHOICES FOR THE FUTURE:
Knowing What's in Your Food Can Help

What we choose to eat and drink affects our whole lives. Knowing what is in your food can help you make healthy choices. However, it can be complicated, as this panel shows.

What's that!

Look at the ingredients in the breadsticks on offer at a popular fast-food restaurant. It is amazing how many ingredients and additives are used in something that one would think was fairly simple!

Breadsticks
Dough: enriched flour (bleached wheat flour, malted barley flour), niacin, ferrous sulfate, thiamin mononitrate (vitamin b1), riboflavin (vitamin b2), folic acid, water, yeast, high fructose corn syrup. Contains 2% or less of each of the following: salt, soybean oil, yeast, datem, ascorbic acid (added as a dough conditioner), whey, vital wheat gluten, azodicarbonamide, mono and diglycerides, sodium stearoyllactylate, enzymes, ascorbic acid. Butter oil: partially hydrogenated soybean oil, lecithin, natural and artificial butter flavor, betacarotene (for color) tbhq [tertiary butyl hydroquinone] and citric acid added to protect flavor and dimethypolysiloxane (an antifoaming agent). Breadstick seasoning: grated parmesan cheese, romano cheese made from cow's milk and other hard grating cheese blend (all from cultured part-skim milk, salt, enzymes, powder cellulose or sodium aluminosillicate added as an anti-caking agent), salt, spices, dehydrated garlic, sodium aluminosillicate added as an anti-caking agent, maltodextrin.

PROBLEMS

Obesity, or being severely overweight, has become a problem among all age groups. Making healthy food choices can help people avoid this. Much of the problem is caused by eating too many high-fat foods and not getting enough exercise. People who are obese run a much greater risk of developing diabetes, heart disease, and arthritis.

▶ Eating too much can lead to health problems.

MAKING YOUR OWN CHOICES

You might make some food choices based on your own feelings or beliefs. Some religions forbid the eating of certain foods or have special rules about the way in which foods are prepared.

Some people become vegetarians because they feel it is wrong to kill animals for food. Others may have strong beliefs about GM foods or do their best to eat only organic food.

▲ A healthy salad can make an excellent snack.

Vegetarians do not eat meat, fish, or seafood, but many are happy to eat animal products, such as milk, cheese, and eggs. Vegans do not eat any foods from animals, including dairy products and honey (made by bees).

Nutritionists agree that a vegetarian diet can be perfectly healthy. Meat contains a lot of protein, so vegetarians and vegans have to make sure they get plenty of protein from other sources. They must also make sure they get enough vitamins and minerals, such as iron (from green vegetables and pulses).

SCARY FUTURE

Scientists at the University of Maryland have reported that it is possible to grow meat in a laboratory. They believe they can take cells from the muscle tissue of a cow or pig and get them to multiply into pieces of beef or pork. The researchers say meat grown in laboratories could be full of nutrients and free of disease. Even vegetarians might eat it because the original cells could be taken from an animal without harming it.

IDEAS FOR HEALTHY EATING

Here are some ideas to help you enjoy healthy eating habits. Forget about dieting or giving up things you love, but try to stick to a few rules. Eat a lot of fruits and vegetables, and make sure there is variety in your diet. Avoid too many pre-prepared meals, and always check the labels first.

▶ A tortilla wrap with vegetables is one example of a healthy lunch.

Quick snacks

✔ Whole-wheat pita bread with **hummus** and lettuce

✔ Tomato and mozzarella on ciabatta bread

✔ Vegetable wrap (tortilla filled with salsa or **guacamole**, chopped cucumber, beans, etc.)

✔ Toasted rye bread with low-fat soft cheese

✔ Mixed salad (tomato, cucumber, lettuce, arugula, spinach, etc.) with oil and lemon dressing and a sprinkling of seeds

✔ Slice of cold pizza, with extra vegetables and a small amount of cheese

✔ Whole-wheat bread with tuna and tomato or chicken and watercress

✔ Whole-wheat bread with chopped chicken, celery, and peanuts

✔ Shredded carrots and cucumber with canned garbanzo beans and lemon juice

✔ Cheese dip with cottage cheese, peppers, cucumber, and herbs eaten with cut raw carrots

More substantial meals

✔ Baked potato with cottage cheese

✔ Grilled chicken breast with green beans, broccoli, and brown rice

✔ Vegetable stir-fry with noodles

✔ Homemade beefburger or beanburger on a bun with sweet corn and green salad

✔ Scrambled eggs with green beans and potato wedges

✔ Baked codfish with roasted sweet corn

✔ Pasta with tomato, zucchini, and mushroom sauce

✔ Pork, beef, or chicken stir-fry with broccoli, peppers, spinach, and noodles

✔ Stuffed pepper, tomato, or zucchini filled with brown rice and nuts

Treats

✔ Cereal or fruit bar made with whole-grain flour, oats, and dried fruit

✔ Dried fruit, apricots, prunes, and apple rings simmered in lemon juice

✔ Strawberry ice cream

✔ Fresh fruit salad made with seasonal fruit

✔ Tropical fruit salad, including pineapple, melon, mangoes, bananas, etc.

✔ Toasted bagel with low-sugar fruit spread

✔ Rice pudding

Tasty drinks

✔ Fruit juice (apple, peach, apricot, etc.)

✔ Freshly squeezed fruit juice (orange, grapefruit)

✔ Vegetable juice (carrot, celery, spinach, etc.)

✔ Fruit and vegetable smoothie (coconut and pineapple, banana and berry, etc.)

✔ Milk and yogurt drink

✔ Herbal tea (camomile, mint, etc.)

✔ Flavored soy milk (for example, chocolate or strawberry flavor)

RECIPES

DATE AND APRICOT CRUMBLE BARS

Forget about those chocolate snacks and bake a healthy alternative! The apricots and dates in these crumble bars are high in vitamins A and B. Apricots have the highest protein content of all dried fruit. Sunflower seeds are rich in protein and minerals, especially potassium.

Ingredients:
1 cup pitted dried dates
1 cup dried apricots,
        roughly cut
1$\frac{1}{3}$ cup regular oats
$\frac{1}{2}$ cup sunflower seeds
$\frac{3}{4}$ cup whole-wheat flour
$\frac{1}{2}$ cup clear honey
$\frac{3}{4}$ cup soy or sunflower oil
$\frac{1}{4}$ cup dried coconut
3 tablespoons orange juice

▲ These are some of the ingredients for date and apricot crumble bars.

Method:
Heat the oven to 350 °F (180 °C).
Line a medium-sized cake pan
with wax paper. Put the dates and apricots in a medium-sized pot and cover with water. Bring to a boil. Then lower the heat and put on the lid. Simmer for fifteen minutes, stirring once or twice, until the apricots are soft and the dates are mushy. Leave to cool. Put the oats, sunflower seeds, and flour into a large bowl or food processor. Add the honey and process at a high speed or mix with a hand-held electric mixer. Gradually stir in the oil and orange juice, beating until combined, to end up with a slightly crumbly mixture. Spread three-quarters of the mixture into the cake pan. Press it down with your hands until it covers the bottom of the pan in an even layer. Make sure to fill the corners. Spread the fruit filling over the top. Mix the coconut into the remaining oat and seed mixture and spread on top of the filling. Bake for 35–40 minutes, until golden brown. Remove from the oven and leave to cool. Cut into sixteen bars.

MERRY BERRY SMOOTHIE

This refreshing smoothie is great for breakfast. You can make smoothies with any fresh or frozen fruits (or vegetables). Add yogurt, skim milk, coconut milk, or chilled fruit juices.

Ingredients:
¹/₂ cup blueberries or raspberries
1 papaya (remove skin and seeds)
1 cup strawberries, washed
1 peeled, frozen banana, cut into ice-cube-sized chunks
1 cup chilled pineapple juice or freshly squeezed orange juice
5-oz container of low-fat natural yogurt
crushed ice
1 teaspoon clear honey (to sweeten)

Method:
Crush three ice cubes (you could do this in a dish towel with a rolling pin). Put these and all the other ingredients, except for the honey, into a blender. Close the lid firmly and blend until smooth. Taste and add honey to sweeten, if required. Drink right away with a friend. Serves two.

▶ The berries in this smoothie are a good source of antioxidants.

GLOSSARY

antibiotic medicine given to people and animals to kill bacteria and control bacterial infections

antioxidant substance that stops certain chemical reactions that cause food to decay

biological to do with living things and the way they grow and act

carbohydrate starch and sugar, found in food, that is converted to glucose when it is digested. The glucose is used for energy.

curdle cause milk to go sour, separate, and become lumpy

DNA (deoxyribonucleic acid) substance in living things that carries genetic information

emulsifier substance that helps ingredients mix, such as oil and water in dough

environmentalist person who cares about and acts to protect the environment, the natural world in which people, animals, and plants live

ferment to break down or start to degrade because of the action of yeast or bacteria

fertilizer chemical or natural substance added to soil to give plants extra nutrients and help them grow

fiber substance in plants that cannot be digested, but that help people to digest food

food chain links between different animals that feed on each other and on plants

fungus group of organisms that includes molds, yeast, and mushrooms

gene basic unit of DNA that passes characteristics from one generation to the next

guacamole avocado mashed with tomato and spiced with chilis

heredity passing on genetic information from one generation to the next

hummus paste of ground garbanzo beans, olive oil, lemon juice, and garlic

import buy goods from another country; the goods are called imports

ingredient substance that makes up part of a dish or recipe

macronutrient substance in food (nutrients) that we need in large amounts, such as carbohydrates, proteins, and fats

micronutrient substance in food (nutrients) that we need in small amounts, such as vitamins and minerals

microorganism microscopic (very tiny) living thing, such as a bacteria

mineral solid chemical substance that occurs naturally in the soil and in food. We need certain minerals in small quantities to be healthy.

mold fungus that causes food to decay. It forms green or black patches on old foods such as bread.

nutrition science that deals with the body taking in and using nutrients in food to stay healthy

obesity being overweight by one-third of the ideal body weight for one's height

organism any living thing

processed food food that has been preserved, colored, frozen, or had chemicals added to it before being sold in stores

protein natural substance made up of amino acids that is needed for strength and growth

publicity something done, such as writing books or giving radio interviews, to make the public aware of something

pulse seed of plants, such as peas, beans, and lentils

radioactivity energy or rays given off by certain radioactive substances that can be harmful to humans

vitamin substance needed in small amounts for normal growth and development

yield amount of food that is produced or grown

FINDING OUT MORE

VISIT A FARM OR A FOOD FACTORY

A real working farm will give you an idea of how food is produced on a small scale. Do not just turn up at a farm and hope for a good reception. Look on the Internet for a list of working farms that are near you. Try contacting your state's Department of Agriculture or your local tourism board. You could also look into visiting a food production line.

LOOK CLOSELY AT LABELS

The next time you are in a grocery store, check out some of the labels and compare different brands for ingredients and nutritional value. Which are the best value for money and which are the most healthy?

BOOKS

Body Needs series: Titles include *Carbohydrates for a Healthy Body, Fats for a Healthy Body, Proteins for a Healthy Body, Vitamins and Minerals for a Healthy Body*, and *Water and Fiber for a Healthy Body*. Chicago: Heinemann Library, 2003. This series looks at what the human body needs to function healthily.

Davidson, Alan. *Penguin Companion to Food*. New York: Penguin, 2002.

Gifford, Clive. *Planet Under Pressure: Pollution*. Chicago: Heinemann Library, 2006.

Kedge, Joanna, and Joanna Watson. *Teen Issues: Diet*. Chicago: Raintree, 2005.

Mason, Paul. *Planet Under Pressure: Food*. Chicago: Heinemann Library, 2006.

Morgan, Sally. *Science at the Edge: Genetic Modification of Foods*. Chicago: Heinemann Library, 2002. Learn more about genetically modified foods.

WEBSITES

www.usda.gov

This is the site of the U.S. Department of Agriculture (USDA), which is responsible for food and nutrition in the United States.

www.fda.gov

This is the site of the U.S. Food and Drug Administration, an agency of the U.S. Department of Health and Human Services.

www.mypyramid.gov

This USDA site offers information on the food guide pyramid, MyPyramid.

www.ams.usda.gov/nop

This section of the USDA website, part of the National Organic Program, offers information on organic food and farming.

www.fao.org

This Food and Agricultural Organization of the United Nations website offers food statistics from around the world.

INDEX